CITIES

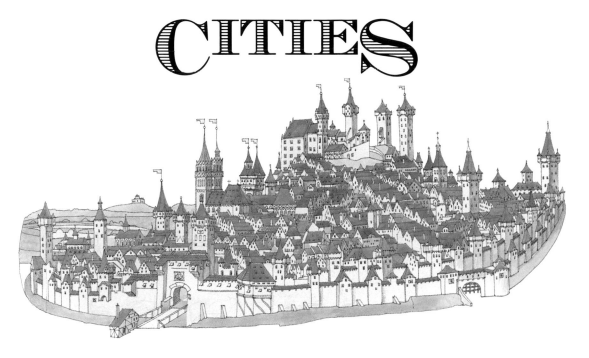

CITIZENS & CIVILISATIONS

Series Editor:
David Salariya was born in Dundee, Scotland, where he studied illustration and printmaking, concentrating on book design in his post-graduate year. He later completed a further post-graduate course in art education at Sussex University. He has illustrated a wide range of books on botanical, historical and mythical subjects. He has designed and created many new series of children's books for publishers in the UK and overseas. In 1989, he established his own publishing company, The Salariya Book Company Ltd. He lives in Brighton with his wife, the illustrator Shirley Willis.

Author:
Fiona Macdonald studied history at Cambridge University and at the University of East Anglia, where she is a part-time Tutor in Medieval History. She has also taught in schools and adult education, and is the author of numerous books for children on historical topics.

Consultant:
Dr Tom Williamson studied history and archeology at Cambridge University, and is now Lecturer in Landscape History at the University of East Anglia. He has written many books and has appeared on radio and television.

Series Editor	David Salariya
Senior Editor	Ruth Taylor
Book Editor	Vicki Power
Consultant	Tom Williamson
Artists	Mark Bergin
	Nick Hewetson
	John James
	Gerald Wood

Artists
Mark Bergin, p 8-9, p 10-11, p 27, p 28, p 34-35, p 42-43; **Nick Hewetson**, p 6-7, p 20-21, p 24-25, p 30-31, p 38-39, p 40-41; **John James**, p 12-13, p 18-19, p 22-23, p 32-33; **Gerald Wood**, p 14-15, p 16-17, p 26, p 29.

First published in 1992
by Watts

Watts
96 Leonard Street
London EC2A 4RH

© The Salariya Book Co Ltd MCMXCII

ISBN 0-7496-0549-9

Printed in Belgium

A CIP catalogue record for this book is available from the British Library.

TIMELINES
CITIES

CITIZENS & CIVILISATIONS

Written by
FIONA MACDONALD

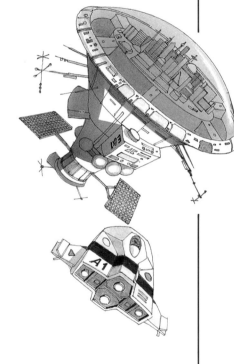

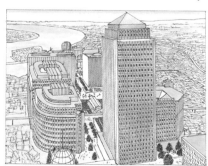

Created & Designed by
DAVID SALARIYA

WATTS

London • New York • Sydney • Toronto

CONTENTS

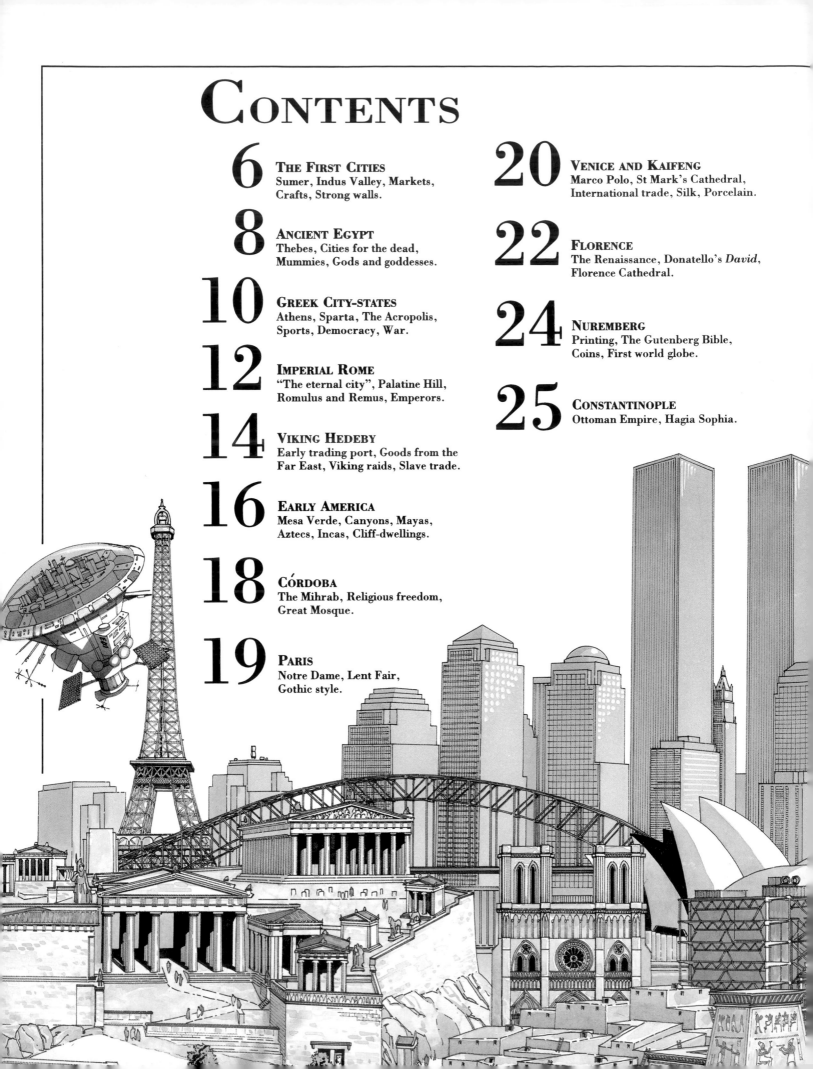

THE FIRST CITIES

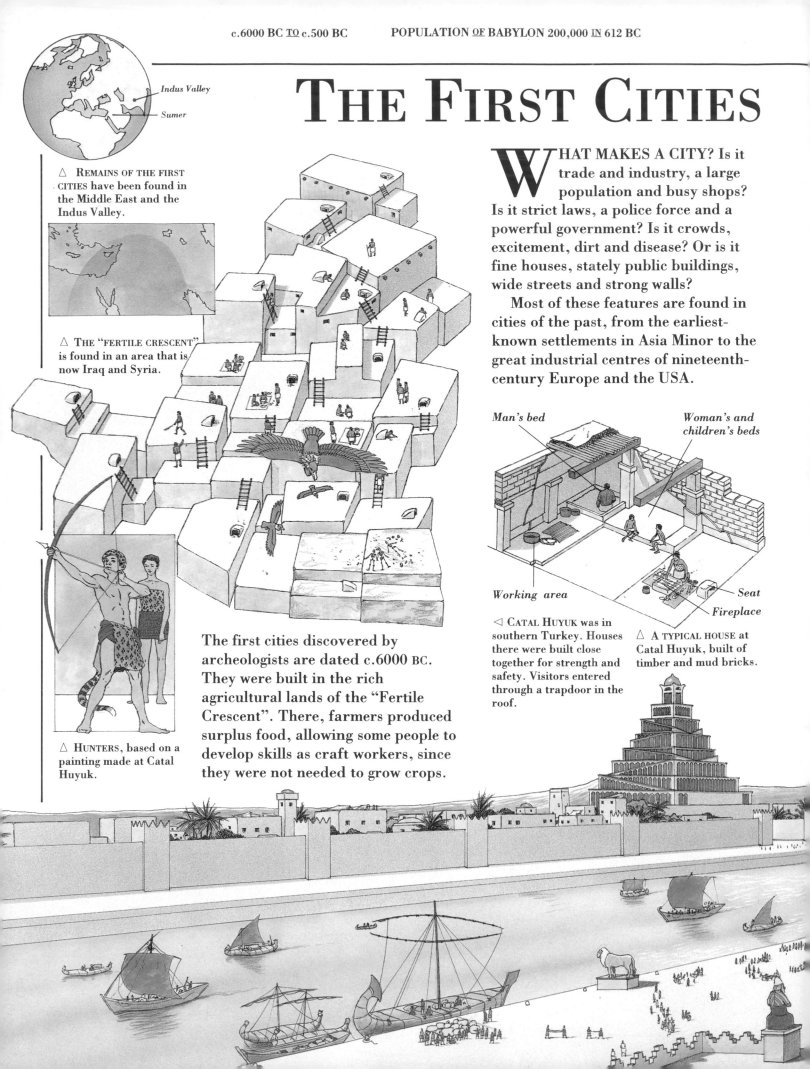

△ REMAINS OF THE FIRST CITIES have been found in the Middle East and the Indus Valley.

△ THE "FERTILE CRESCENT" is found in an area that is now Iraq and Syria.

△ HUNTERS, based on a painting made at Catal Huyuk.

WHAT MAKES A CITY? Is it trade and industry, a large population and busy shops? Is it strict laws, a police force and a powerful government? Is it crowds, excitement, dirt and disease? Or is it fine houses, stately public buildings, wide streets and strong walls?

Most of these features are found in cities of the past, from the earliest-known settlements in Asia Minor to the great industrial centres of nineteenth-century Europe and the USA.

Man's bed

Woman's and children's beds

Working area

Seat

Fireplace

◁ CATAL HUYUK was in southern Turkey. Houses there were built close together for strength and safety. Visitors entered through a trapdoor in the roof.

△ A TYPICAL HOUSE at Catal Huyuk, built of timber and mud bricks.

The first cities discovered by archeologists are dated c.6000 BC. They were built in the rich agricultural lands of the "Fertile Crescent". There, farmers produced surplus food, allowing some people to develop skills as craft workers, since they were not needed to grow crops.

△ GOING TO MARKET in Sumer, c.2500 BC. Merchants carry barley, fish, mutton and wool.

▷ MARKET AT THE GATES OF EBLA, a major Sumerian city. Crops grew outside the walls.

Busy centres grew up, where foodstuffs and the new, manufactured goods were exchanged. Farmers came to exchange their surplus produce for items that they could not make themselves. Craft workers settled nearby, so that they could trade with travelling merchants who supplied them with the raw materials they needed. They surrounded their homes with high, protective walls.

△ SUMER was located between the Tigris and Euphrates rivers in present-day Iraq. The Sumerians left records of their lives in writing that is called "cuneiform".

▽ THE ROYAL PALACE at Babylon, built by King Nebuchadnezzar II (reigned 604–562 BC), who erected many other great buildings and monuments.

This way of life continued for thousands of years. In time, cities became larger and better planned, with palaces, temples, gardens, fresh water supplies and simple sanitation. Taxes paid for this and for the police. Laws were made; the earliest that survive were drawn up in c.2000 BC by King Hammurabi. They laid down rules for good behaviour by all.

△ IMPRESSIVE HOUSES and paved streets in the Indus Valley city of Mohenjo-Daro, c.2500 BC, in an area that is now in Pakistan. The Indus cities traded with Babylon by sea.

ANCIENT EGYPT

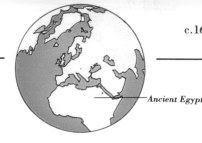

Ancient Egypt

△ EGYPTIANS LIVED on the banks of the Nile.

▽ WALL PAINTING of a market. Goods being exchanged include sandals, fish and cakes.

THE EGYPTIAN RULING DYNASTIES were strong and powerful. Pharaohs and priests controlled a vast kingdom, stretching from the Mediterranean Sea to present-day Sudan. Ancient Egyptian architecture echoed this power. Temples and palaces were built from huge blocks of granite and sandstone; their entrances were guarded by colossal statues of animals, gods and men. These mighty buildings were constructed by teams of skilful workmen, paid by taxes collected from citizens. These workmen, and other ordinary Egyptians, lived in houses made of mud bricks, dried in the sun. Unlike the pharaohs' stone-built monuments, most of these simple houses have not survived.

Egyptian cities were large, compared with other ancient cities. Thebes, the capital during the years of Egypt's greatest power, was said to have a hundred gates. This may not be accurate, but it tells us a lot about the city's former fame.

▽ TEMPLE, BUILT c.1500 BC. Egyptian priests taught that a god's spirit visited his temple each day.

Pylon (gateway)

Public courtyard

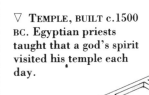

Private hall (used by priests)

Holy shrine

▷ TOWN HOUSE OF A NOBLE FAMILY, c.1400 BC. Homes like these were furnished with beds, tables and chairs, and decorated with wall paintings, glassware and pottery.

Cool work-space on roof

Reed awning

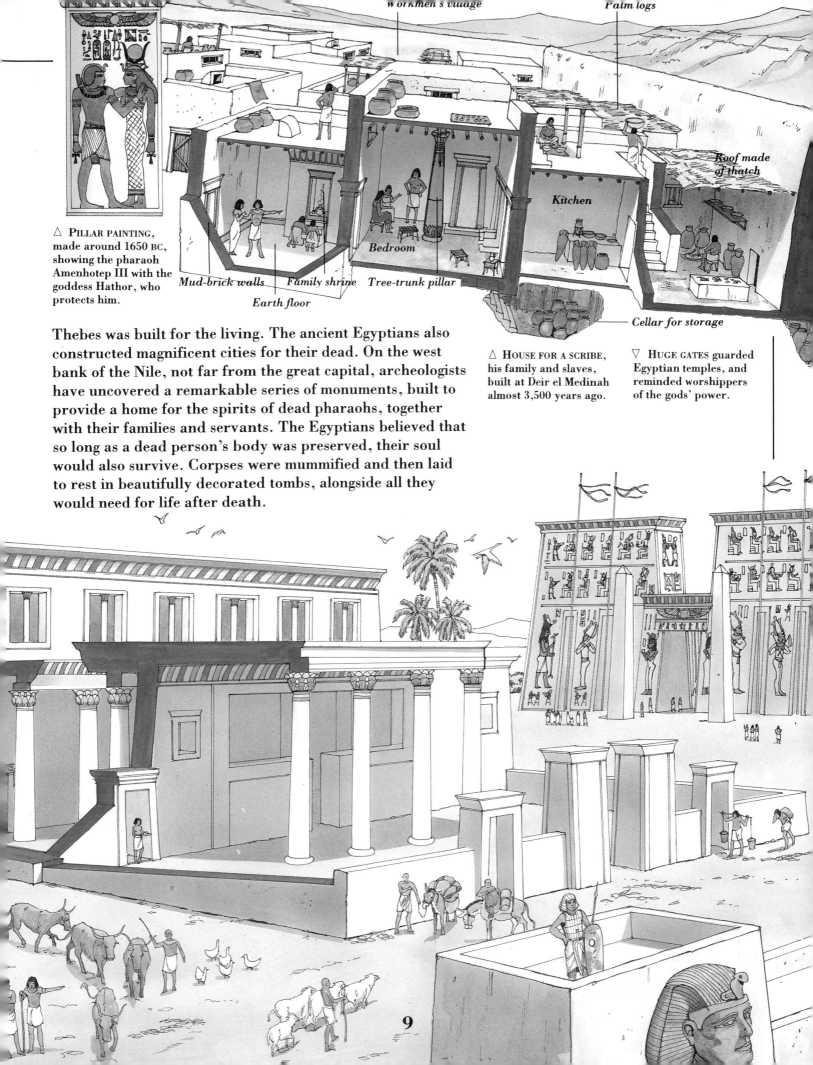

Roof made
of thatch

Kitchen

Bedroom

△ PILLAR PAINTING,
made around 1650 BC,
showing the pharaoh
Amenhotep III with the
goddess Hathor, who
protects him.

Mud-brick walls   Family shrine   Tree-trunk pillar

Earth floor

Cellar for storage

Thebes was built for the living. The ancient Egyptians also
constructed magnificent cities for their dead. On the west
bank of the Nile, not far from the great capital, archeologists
have uncovered a remarkable series of monuments, built to
provide a home for the spirits of dead pharaohs, together
with their families and servants. The Egyptians believed that
so long as a dead person's body was preserved, their soul
would also survive. Corpses were mummified and then laid
to rest in beautifully decorated tombs, alongside all they
would need for life after death.

△ HOUSE FOR A SCRIBE,
his family and slaves,
built at Deir el Medinah
almost 3,500 years ago.

▽ HUGE GATES guarded
Egyptian temples, and
reminded worshippers
of the gods' power.

9

GREEK CITY-STATES

MAN WAS DESIGNED BY NATURE TO LIVE IN A CITY-STATE. That is what one famous Greek philosopher taught his students. Why did he think life there was so good? Greek city-states were independent territories. Some, like Corinth, were weak; others, like Sparta, dominated surrounding lands.

Each city-state contained a fortified town. The strongest also had access to the sea, to provide fish, salt, and the chance of foreign trade.

▽ THE CITY OF ATHENS lay between the sea and the mountains, close to a fine harbour.

▽ ATHENIAN CRAFTSMEN and traders at work, from pottery made in the city, c.450 BC. Clay was dug near the city and carried to the potters' workshops. The finished pots were highly prized.

City-states were quarrelsome, competitive, and jealous of their own rights. Each made its own laws and had its own army. Athens was the most famous city-state. Its system of government was admired by many people in the ancient world and is still influential today.

Athens was a democracy. All free adult male citizens (though not women or slaves) had the duty to take part in the government. They discussed plans and policies in the assembly and voted to elect leaders. They also served in the military and law courts.

Potter　　*Sculptor*　　*Fishmonger*　　*Shoemaker*

▷ GREEK metalworkers making statues.

▽ THE ACROPOLIS (strong fortress) was sited on a high cliff in the centre of Athens. The citizens built many beautiful temples there.

Each temple was the "home" of a god. It contained a splendid statue and other holy objects. Traditionally, people came to the temples on festival days to make sacrifices to the gods and ask for their help. The fine new temples also showed how rich their city was.

▷ THE MOST FAMOUS BUILDING on the Acropolis was the Parthenon (*right*), dedicated to the goddess Athena.

KEY
1 Parthenon.
2 Grand entrance.
3 Treasury.
4 Temple of Victory.
5 Temple for old statue of Athena.
6 Site of original shrine of Athena.
7 Altar.
8 Sanctuary of Artemis.
9 Treasury to keep valuable offerings.
10 House of temple maidens and priestesses.
11 Temple of Zeus.

City-states were centres of trade, industry, and religion. Farmers brought olive oil, wine, bread, cheese and honey to sell in city markets. Athenian pottery was famous; other city-states were well-known for their textiles and metalwork. There were festival processions, linked to sports and plays, to honour each city's protecting god. Education was very important. For freeborn boys, there were excellent schools and academies.

It was indeed a good life for some. The privileged citizens relied on slaves and servants to care for them.

▷ ALL BUILDINGS date from after 479 BC, when the Acropolis was attacked by invaders.

11

IMPERIAL ROME

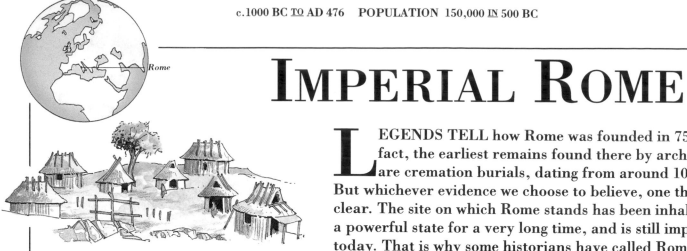

LEGENDS TELL how Rome was founded in 753 BC. In fact, the earliest remains found there by archeologists are cremation burials, dating from around 1000 BC. But whichever evidence we choose to believe, one thing is clear. The site on which Rome stands has been inhabited by a powerful state for a very long time, and is still important today. That is why some historians have called Rome "the eternal city".

At first, Rome was governed by kings. Then it became a republic, ruled by elected officials. The city became powerful, and ruled over a wide territory. In 27 BC, this was declared an empire, led by the first Roman Emperor, Augustus.

△ THE EARLIEST ROMAN BUILDINGS were simple wooden huts, like these from the Palatine Hill, built c.800 BC.

▽ THE GREAT CITY OF ROME sprawled across seven low hills overlooking the River Tiber in central Italy.

Under the Empire, Rome grew in power and, by AD c.100, ruled over territory stretching from Scotland to Africa and the borders of Asia. Rome was capital of half the known world.

The emperors had beautiful new buildings constructed. Temples, palaces, markets and public baths were all rebuilt. Aqueducts brought fresh water, and drains carried sewage away. Huge arenas were built, where citizens watched chariot races and gladiator fights. Monuments celebrated the victories of Roman generals and their troops. Wealthy citizens built fine new houses and filled them with furniture, paintings and sculpture. Ordinary people lived in crowded blocks of flats, or above inns and workshops.

△ SCULPTURE of a wolf, said to have raised human twins Romulus and Remus, who later founded Rome.

△ ROMAN EMPERORS issued coins decorated with their portraits. This example shows Augustus (27 BC-AD 14).

△ SENATORS HELPED TO RUN THE GOVERNMENT of Rome and its empire. They came from wealthy families.

△ CARVED TOMBSTONES TELL us about daily life in imperial Rome. This fragment portrays a greengrocer's shop.

△ THIS TOMBSTONE SHOWS an ironmonger's stall. Metal knives and hooks hang on the wall, ready for sale.

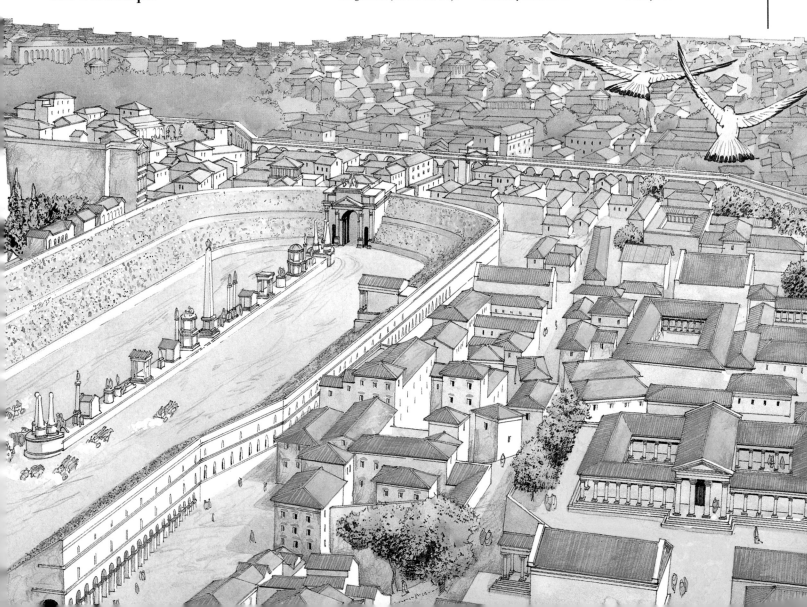

VIKING HEDEBY

△ DENMARK was ruled by Vikings from the 7th to the 11th centuries. Vikings also controlled Norway and Sweden.

△ HEDEBY was founded by King Godfred of Denmark at the head of the Slie fjord, on a major trading route between the North Sea and the Baltic Sea.

TODAY, MANY PEOPLE THINK of the Vikings as bloodthirsty warriors, swooping in from the sea to attack peaceful towns and villages. During the seventh to the eleventh centuries, there were frequent Viking raids on wealthy settlements throughout northern Europe. The Vikings brought death and destruction whenever they attacked. But these terrifying raids were only part of the Viking story. Many Viking expeditions were peaceful. The Vikings were also great traders and travelled widely seeking goods to buy and sell.

The port of Hedeby is one of the best-known Viking settlements. Craftsmen (especially metalworkers), shipbuilders, money changers, slave traders, fishermen, fur trappers, brewers, cooks and provision merchants all made a living from the profits of trade.

△ LUXURY GOODS from distant lands were sold at Hedeby. This flask, bowl and cup came from the Middle East.

△ COIN from Hedeby.

Craftsmen used whalebone as a raw material.

Dead cow above door as offering to the gods.

Shipbuilders

Blacksmith

Sledge

Stream supplied drinking water.

Cows

Pigs

△ INSIDE A VIKING HOUSE. The walls were made of timber, wattle and daub; the roof was thatched. A central hearth provided heat.

Furniture was very simple: wooden benches and storage chests. Straw mattresses covered with rugs were used for beds.

Hedeby was an international market centre. It lay close to long-distance overland trade routes linking the Viking territories with Russia, Constantinople and the Middle East. Viking merchants made the difficult journey to these faraway lands to sell silks, spices, glassware, jewels and pottery. In return, they purchased slaves (prisoners captured in Viking raids), walrus ivory, amber, salt, weapons and furs.

Hedeby was almost completely destroyed by fire in c.1050. Its great days as a Viking port were over.

△ SKELETON OF A RICH MAN, buried at Birka, another Viking trading town. His goods, buried with him, include his weapons and horse.

Loom

Bench

Stockade

Rampart

Merchant ship (knorr)

Toilet

Smoke filtered through thatched roof.

Slave traders

Thatched roof

Merchants

15

Wattle and daub

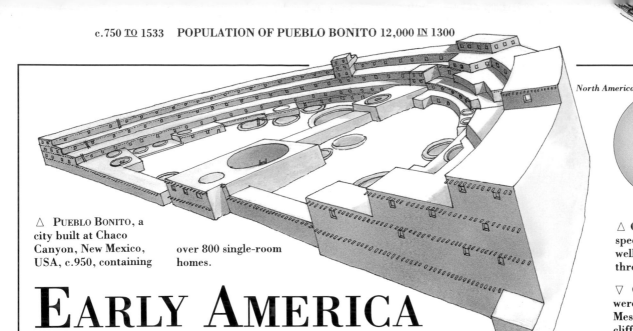

△ PUEBLO BONITO, a city built at Chaco Canyon, New Mexico, USA, c.950, containing over 800 single-room homes.

North America

South America

△ CITIES were built at spectacular, well-defended sites throughout America.

▽ OVER 200 HOUSES were built at the foot of Mesa Verde's sheltering cliff. The inhabitants abandoned their city around 1300, possibly because of a water shortage.

EARLY AMERICA

THE AMERICAN LANDSCAPE is vast and varied. Living conditions range from snowy mountains to tropical rainforests. Some regions, like the canyon lands of the North American west, are deserts, where temperatures can be extremely hot or bitterly cold. Others, like the central lake area of Mexico, are swamps. All of them present enormous challenges to would-be city builders.

▽ CLIFF PALACE, Mesa Verde, in Colorado, USA, built c.1150.

On these pages, you can see how some of these environmental challenges were overcome by American peoples between c.750 and 1533. Several remarkable styles of architecture developed, reflecting different ways of life and varying religious beliefs.

Some of the most impressive North American cities were built in the desert. No written evidence survives to tell us what life there was like, but the remains suggest that the desert cities were prosperous and well organised. Citizens lived close together, for safety, companionship, and to encourage trade. Maize, beans and pumpkins were grown in irrigated fields; small mammals were hunted for food. Pottery, knives and jewellery from Pueblo Bonito and Mesa Verde have been found over a wide area, suggesting that these cities had set up trading links far beyond their walls.

▷ THE AZTEC CAPITAL CITY of Tenochtitlán rose to power between 1325 and 1519.

△ MAYA NOBLEMAN, c.750, ready to play in the sacred ball game played in many early American cities. He wears padded clothes and jewellery.

The American ball game was more than a sport. It could be a matter of life and death. Sometimes the loser was killed as a sacrifice to the gods.

△ THE INCA EMPIRE GREW RICH through gifts from conquered peoples. Here, messengers bring cloth, cloaks, lace and golden cups as a tribute.

▷ THE INCA CAPITAL CITY was built at Cuzco, high above sea level in the Andes Mountains. It flourished for less than 200 years between 1350 and 1533.

▽ THE TOWERING PYRAMID, or Great Temple, was dedicated to the god of war Huitzilopochtli and to Tlaloc, the god of rain.

In South America, great cities were built by the Maya people in Guatemala, by the Aztecs in Mexico, and by the Incas in the mountains of Peru. Using simple technology, the city builders constructed temples, palaces and fortifications on difficult sites.

▽ THE GREAT AZTEC TEMPLE PRECINCT also had smaller shrines, a college for priests and a sacred ball court.

CÓRDOBA

△ CÓRDOBA, in southern Spain, became the capital of lands under Muslim rule.

△ MUSLIMS AND CHRISTIANS play chess. From a 13th-century manuscript.

△ THE MIHRAB (niche showing the direction of Mecca) in the Great Mosque at Córdoba. It is decorated with beautiful tiles.

CÓRDOBA WAS FAMOUS as the city where people from three different faiths lived together peacefully. It was ruled by Muslim caliphs, and many of its inhabitants were Muslims. Many Christian and Jewish people lived there, too. Remarkably for the time, the caliphs allowed them freedom of worship. They also permitted scholars and religious teachers to study and debate.

Ordinary citizens mixed freely. (In the rest of Europe, Jews and Muslims were kept apart from the Christian majority.) Craftsmen were employed for their skills, not for their beliefs, and designed many beautiful buildings in a new, Spanish-Muslim style. Poets, musicians and philosophers of all three faiths were welcome at the Muslim court. Each faith contributed to Córdoba's lively civilisation.

△ WALL PAINTING showing medieval Muslim courtiers, from the palace at Granada.

They seem to be deep in discussion – favourite court topics included love, hunting and war.

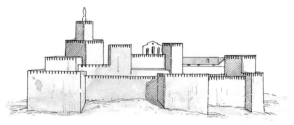

△ CHRISTIAN TROOPS captured Córdoba in 1236. From then until 1492, the city of

Granada was capital of Muslim Spain. Many fine buildings still survive from that time.

▽ THE GREAT MOSQUE at Córdoba, built c.900, and admired as a marvel of medieval Muslim architecture.

PARIS

MEDIEVAL PARIS was the capital of one of the most powerful nations in Europe. The city's wealth was based on trade and its connections with the royal and noble families who governed France. Citizens and nobles built palaces and churches in the new "gothic" style.

By 1300, Paris had become famous as a centre of learning. Scholars and churchmen from all over Europe came to live in the city, to study and to teach. Students attended lectures, sat up all night drinking, danced, sang and became involved in fights.

△ MEDIEVAL PARIS grew on the site of early Celtic and Roman settlements in France.

△ THE LENT FAIR brought merchants and travellers to Paris in the Middle Ages.

◁ PARIS IN THE 15TH CENTURY, as shown in a contemporary manuscript illustration.

Paris has always been a leader of fashion, attracting top architects and designers. By 1400, they had transformed the city's skyline with tall towers and soaring steeples.

▽ BRONZE SEAL, designed in 1896 to commemorate the founding of Paris University in 1215.

▷ VIEW FROM THE ROOF of Notre Dame Cathedral in the heart of Paris. Building started in 1163. The cathedral contains many fine medieval carvings and glowing stained-glass windows.

VENICE AND KAIFENG

THE PROUD CITY OF VENICE grew up on an unpromising site: unstable, unhealthy, foggy and waterlogged. Yet, by the 13th century, Venetian merchants were among the most prosperous in Europe, and the Venetian fleet controlled a wide empire including Greece, Cyprus, and islands off the Turkish coast. Venetian ships linked customers at home with the producers of rare, exotic goods in Turkey, China and the East.

△ VENICE WAS BUILT around a marshy lagoon beside the Adriatic Sea in Italy.

△ GIOVANNI MOCENIGO, doge (ruler) of Venice in the 15th century.

△ LETTERBOX where Venetians could post anonymous complaints about their enemies to the government.

△ A VENETIAN GALLEY, used for trade and warfare, equipped with sails and oars.

Merchants like Marco Polo admired the wealthy, comfortable and well-run Chinese cities they visited on their travels. Kaifeng was one of the most important trading centres in northern China. Its craft workers produced silks, paper, dyestuffs and fine porcelain, which were highly prized by European purchasers.

◁ A STREET SCENE IN KAIFENG, the capital of Sung China, from a scroll painted c.1120. A busy industrial centre, Kaifeng had over 260,000 households and perhaps a million people, making it larger than any Western city at this date.

Venice was a republic, governed by wealthy citizens, not by a king. The doge was head of state; he was elected, and held office for life. Venetian citizens valued their freedom. This independent spirit often led to bitter quarrels, but, on the whole, disputes and intrigues were not allowed to interfere with the all-important business of making money.

Civic pride was encouraged by the sight of handsome new buildings, like St Mark's Church and the doge's palace nearby. The government also won support by arranging festivals and processions for citizens to enjoy.

One of the most famous Venetian merchants was Marco Polo, who travelled to the court of the Great Khan in China at the end of the 13th century. The book describing his travels was a medieval best-seller and is still popular today.

◁ ST MARK'S was the most splendid church in Venice, and the piazza (square) outside was the centre of public life. It was used for ceremonies, festivals and as a market place.

△ FLORENCE LIES in the valley of the River Arno, which flows through central Italy.

△ MOSAIC PANEL showing the city's coat of arms.

▷ GOODS FOR SALE in a street market c.1550 included silk, shoes, weapons and food.

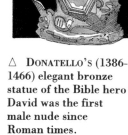

△ DONATELLO'S (1386-1466) elegant bronze statue of the Bible hero David was the first male nude since Roman times.

▽ GOLD FLORIN COIN, weighing 3.5 grams. It was decorated with pictures of lilies and of St John the Baptist.

△ FLORENTINE FLORIN.

FLORENCE

THE CITY AS A WORK OF ART. That is how one famous historian described the Italian city of Florence during the Renaissance, in the fifteenth and early sixteenth centuries.

▽ PANORAMIC VIEW of Florence, based on a painting by Vasari, made in 1530. It shows the city surrounded by great walls.

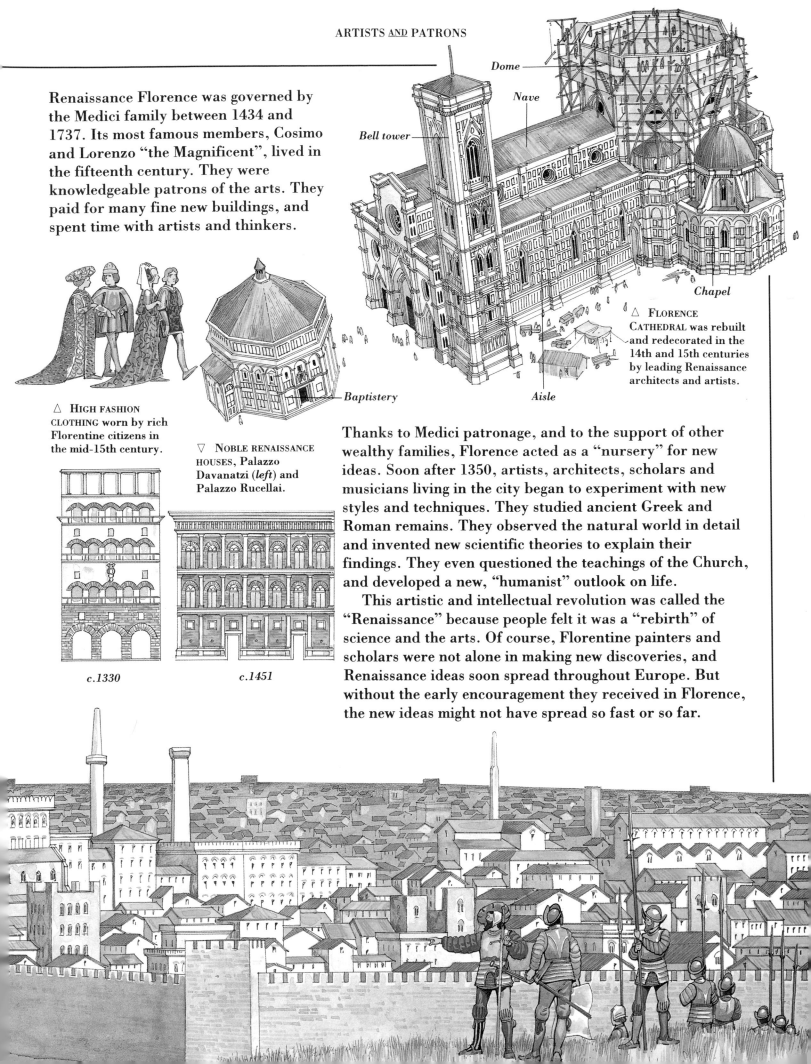

Renaissance Florence was governed by the Medici family between 1434 and 1737. Its most famous members, Cosimo and Lorenzo "the Magnificent", lived in the fifteenth century. They were knowledgeable patrons of the arts. They paid for many fine new buildings, and spent time with artists and thinkers.

Dome

Nave

Bell tower

Chapel

△ FLORENCE CATHEDRAL was rebuilt and redecorated in the 14th and 15th centuries by leading Renaissance architects and artists.

Aisle

Baptistery

△ HIGH FASHION CLOTHING worn by rich Florentine citizens in the mid-15th century.

▽ NOBLE RENAISSANCE HOUSES, Palazzo Davanatzi (*left*) and Palazzo Rucellai.

c.1330

c.1451

Thanks to Medici patronage, and to the support of other wealthy families, Florence acted as a "nursery" for new ideas. Soon after 1350, artists, architects, scholars and musicians living in the city began to experiment with new styles and techniques. They studied ancient Greek and Roman remains. They observed the natural world in detail and invented new scientific theories to explain their findings. They even questioned the teachings of the Church, and developed a new, "humanist" outlook on life.

This artistic and intellectual revolution was called the "Renaissance" because people felt it was a "rebirth" of science and the arts. Of course, Florentine painters and scholars were not alone in making new discoveries, and Renaissance ideas soon spread throughout Europe. But without the early encouragement they received in Florence, the new ideas might not have spread so fast or so far.

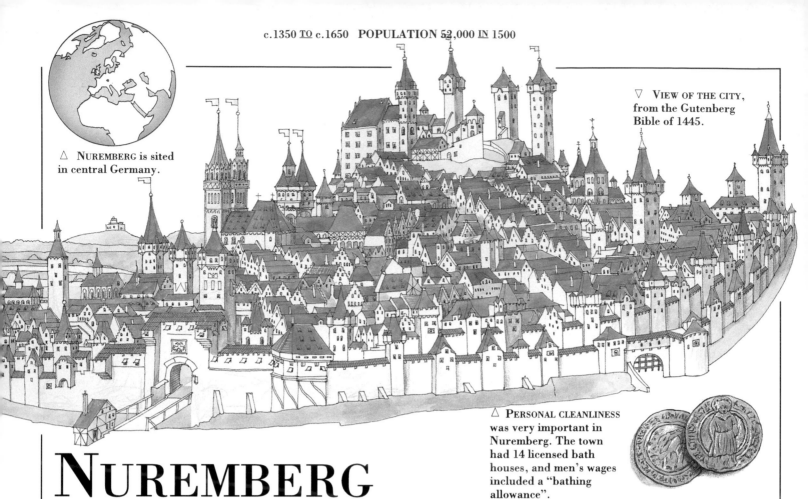

△ NUREMBERG is sited in central Germany.

▽ VIEW OF THE CITY, from the Gutenberg Bible of 1445.

NUREMBERG

△ PERSONAL CLEANLINESS was very important in Nuremberg. The town had 14 licensed bath houses, and men's wages included a "bathing allowance".

△ NUREMBERG GOLD COIN, c.1500, reveals the metalworkers' skill.

NOT FAR FROM NUREMBERG, miners toiled deep underground in dark, dangerous tunnels. They were searching for iron and silver, which had been known to exist in the area since Roman times. Fortunately for their purses, although unfortunately for their health, they found large deposits of both minerals. Nuremberg's metalworkers – and citizens who sold goods to them – would now grow rich.

△ SELF-PORTRAIT, c.1498, by Albrecht Dürer, the most famous German artist of the Renaissance.

◁ PRINTING WITH MOVEABLE TYPE was invented by Johann Gutenberg in Nuremberg during the 15th century. (The Chinese had a similar technique, but it was unknown in the West.)

△ MAINZ BIBLE, 1450, from Nuremberg.

▽ THE FIRST WORLD GLOBE was made in Nuremberg in 1492. It does not show America, because Columbus had not yet returned from his voyage of discovery to the New World.

Fifteenth-century craftsmen in Nuremberg were famous for coins, locks and other fine metal objects. But in 1445, Johann Gutenberg had the idea of using metalwork skills in a new way. He printed a book, using moveable letters cast from molten metal. As we now know, Gutenberg's invention was to change the world.

△ WEALTHY CITIZENS dressed up to attend church on a Sunday, from 15th-century drawings by Dürer.

PANORAMA showing the site of Constantinople and its impressive buildings, from a 16th-century book.

◁ SULTAN SULEIMAN THE MAGNIFICENT, 1520-66, ruled over the Ottoman Empire at its most powerful.

▽ HAGIA SOPHIA was built as a Christian church in 537. Then, it had the world's largest dome. It was turned into a mosque in 1453, when Turkish troops captured the city.

▽ GREAT MOSQUE OF HAGIA SOPHIA (Holy Wisdom) in Constantinople.

CONSTANTINOPLE

CONSTANTINOPLE, now Istanbul, is a city that men have fought and died for. For Europeans, it is the gateway to the east. For invading troops from Asia, it guards the overland route into Europe. Over the centuries, the city was ruled by Romans, Greeks and Turks. After 1453, it became the capital of the Muslim Ottoman Empire. During the sixteenth century, the Ottoman rulers enriched it with many fine new buildings. The architect Sinan designed mosques, palaces and gardens in Muslim style.

Constantinople was a fortress city, and was guarded by strong walls. It also had a large civilian population. They were well-served by coffee shops, markets and bazaars.

▷ CONSTANTINOPLE stands where Europe meets Asia, on the shores of the Black Sea.

▽ TURKISH TROOPS, c.1650.

AMSTERDAM

△ AMSTERDAM was the capital city of the Netherlands, in northwestern Europe.

△ SEAL, 1654.

IN 1609, THE REPUBLIC OF THE NETHERLANDS won independence from Spain. Its capital, Amsterdam, was already a thriving port. Now the inhabitants wanted to rebuild the city as a monument to their own serious and sober beliefs. The surviving evidence suggests that Dutch architects fulfilled this aim. Seventeenth-century buildings in Amsterdam are solid, well-built, calm, comfortable and discreet. There is nothing extravagant or vulgar about them. The city became a pleasant, respectable and (for the merchants) profitable place to live. Parks and gardens created healthy open spaces. Church spires towered above the houses, revealing the citizens' sturdy Protestant faith.

△ EAST INDIA HOUSE, headquarters of the Dutch East India Company, which imported cloth, spices and porcelain from the Far East.

▽ TYPICAL DUTCH TOWNHOUSE, c.1650, built several storeys high to save space.

▽ FIRES WERE FREQUENT in cities when houses were built of wood. After many fires in the 15th century, Amsterdam was rebuilt in brick.

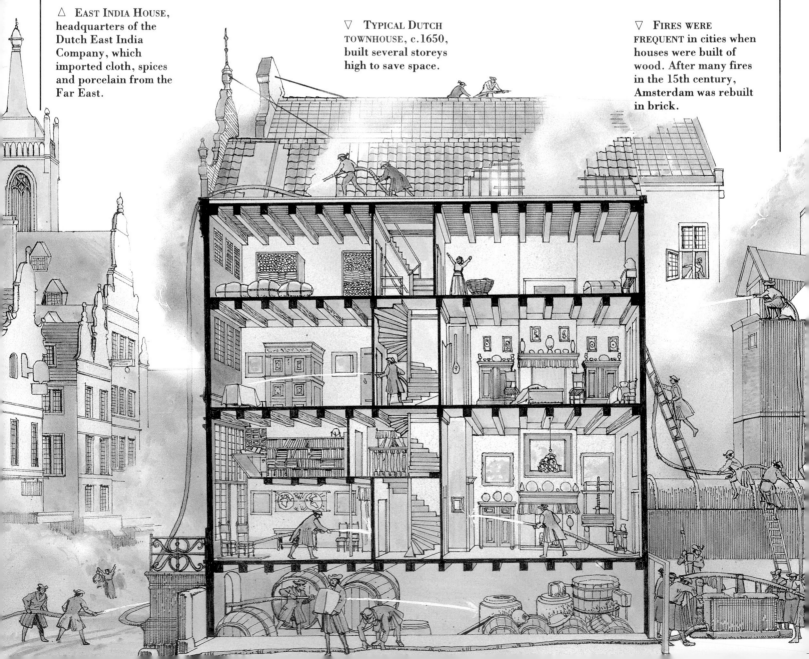

VIENNA

AMONG CAPITAL CITIES, Vienna had a reputation for ease and enjoyment. This is not strictly fair, of course. Like any eighteenth-century city, Vienna had problems. Cramped living conditions led to epidemic disease. There was crime and unemployment. But for many carefree people, Vienna was a charming and "civilised" place to live.

△ VIENNA WAS THE CAPITAL of the Austro-Hungarian Empire in Europe.

△ THEATRE IN VIENNA, where fashionable audiences flocked to see all the latest plays.

△ THE PALACE OF SCHÖNBRUNN, built between 1695 and 1700 on the edge of Vienna.

It was designed in elaborate style and surrounded by well-planned gardens.

△ OPERA was a popular entertainment among wealthy citizens.

Singers performed works by modern composers like Mozart.

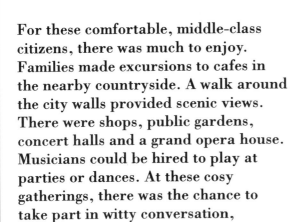

For these comfortable, middle-class citizens, there was much to enjoy. Families made excursions to cafes in the nearby countryside. A walk around the city walls provided scenic views. There were shops, public gardens, concert halls and a grand opera house. Musicians could be hired to play at parties or dances. At these cosy gatherings, there was the chance to take part in witty conversation, flirtation or political intrigue.

▽ CRAFT WORKERS made luxury goods for wealthy Viennese customers, who wanted elegant silverware, padded furniture and patterned silks.

▽ GLASSBLOWER shaping dishes.

▽ SCENE IN A FACTORY making fine porcelain.

▽ WEAVING SILK and woollen fabrics.

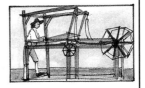

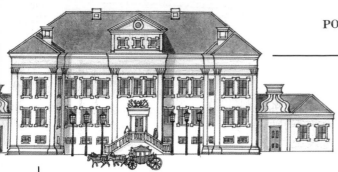

ST PETERSBURG

TSAR PETER "THE GREAT" OF RUSSIA was a man of grand passions and desires. One of his most cherished projects was to build a complete new city on an extremely inhospitable site. Although the human cost was appalling – more than 150,000 building workers died – Tsar Peter had good reasons for his choice. The new city would be a port, enabling the Russian navy to attack ships from neighbouring lands. It would also be easier for him to control rebellious nobles in this remote new city, where they would be far from their family estates.

Peter wanted his city to be majestic and beautiful. The palaces built there are elegant and luxurious, but, nearby, many ordinary citizens lived (and died) in cold, squalid hovels.

△ THE FIRST WINTER PALACE was built for Tsar Peter the Great between 1716 and 1725.

Unlike earlier Russian palaces, it was designed in Italian rather than purely Russian style.

▽ ST PETERSBURG was built on marshy ground on the shores of the Baltic Sea.

△ IN WINTER, the seas froze; in summer, fevers caused many deaths.

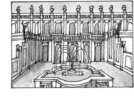

△ THE PETERHOF, Tsar Peter's house.

◁ PETER THE GREAT admired Western ideas and Western fashions. He forced Russian men to cut off their beards, as part of his plan to make Russia more like Western Europe.

△ TSAR PETER THE GREAT (ruled 1682 - 1725) was 2 metres tall.

▽ THE PORT OF ST PETERSBURG also catered for many merchant ships bringing foods, timber and furs from lands around the Baltic sea.

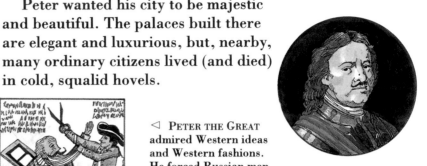

PARIS

△ IN 1789, PARIS was the second largest city in Europe, after London. It had tripled in size since 1700.

▽ THE OLD BUILDINGS of medieval Paris were torn down to make way for a series of broad new avenues, known as boulevards. Several lead outward, in star formation, from this central open space.

FOR FRANCE, the late eighteenth century was a time of turmoil. After the Revolution of 1789, there was war before Napoleon Bonaparte crowned himself Emperor in 1804. He set about restoring France to her former glory. As well as fighting off enemy attacks, this also meant rebuilding Paris to turn it into a modern capital worthy of the Emperor and all he had achieved. Napoleon did not live to see his grand projects finished, but the rebuilding of Paris was continued by the city's leaders. Under the direction of Baron Haussmann (1809-91), over 30,000 homes were demolished and people rehoused to make way for roads, markets and monuments. Haussmann's schemes changed the face of Paris, and many of his buildings survive today.

△ THE MIGHTY ARC DE TRIOMPHE was designed to commemorate the French Emperor Napoleon's victories in battle. It is 50 metres high and 45 metres wide. Building started in 1806 and was completed in 1836.

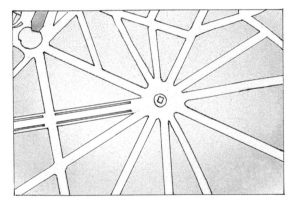

▷ THE CHURCH OF LA MADELEINE was made like an ancient Greek temple. It was built between 1764 and 1842.

▽ VISITING THE UNDERGROUND TUNNELS of the city's new sewers became a popular excursion for tourists in 19th-century Paris.

Haussmann planned the new Paris to look magnificent, but also to work well. His elegant boulevards were lined with handsome shops, but they were also wide enough to allow the army to march quickly to any trouble spot. Haussmann also built five new bridges and encouraged the development of the first Paris railway, which opened in 1837.

▽ VIEW ALONG A BOULEVARD. Citizens and visitors all enjoyed strolling down these elegant new streets.

NEW YORK GROWS

NEW YORK WAS FOUNDED IN 1626, on land purchased from a group of American Indians by the Dutch West India Company. They exchanged cloth, trinkets and beads worth 60 Dutch guilders for 20,000 acres of land. New York (initially Fort Amsterdam) began as a wooden "castle" surrounded by flimsy houses. Climatic conditions were not favourable for growing crops, and inhabitants were attacked by British, French and Swedish troops. For many years, the city covered only a small area at the tip of Manhattan Island. Wall Street, now the city's financial district, follows the line of the wall that marked the city boundary until it was demolished in 1767. Wall Street was also the site of the slave market.

In 1811, the now well-known grid pattern of streets was designed to allow for expansion. By 1871, New York's population topped one million.

△ THE FIRST SETTLEMENT IN NEW YORK was Dutch, called Fort Amsterdam.

Buildings included the fort, 30 houses for Dutch settlers, and a tall windmill.

△ BY 1664, THE FORT was surrendered to the English and renamed New York. By this time, more than 7,000 people, mostly Europeans, had settled there.

△ THIS SEAL was fixed to official documents of Fort Amsterdam after 1654, when settlers won the right to make their own laws.

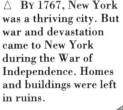

△ BY 1767, New York was a thriving city. But war and devastation came to New York during the War of Independence. Homes and buildings were left in ruins.

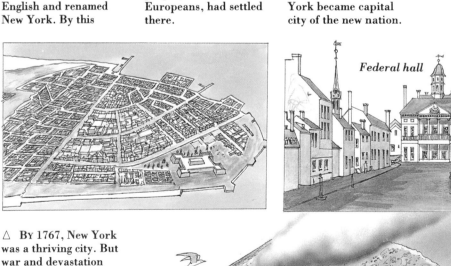

▽ AFTER THE WAR OF INDEPENDENCE, New York became capital city of the new nation.

Federal hall

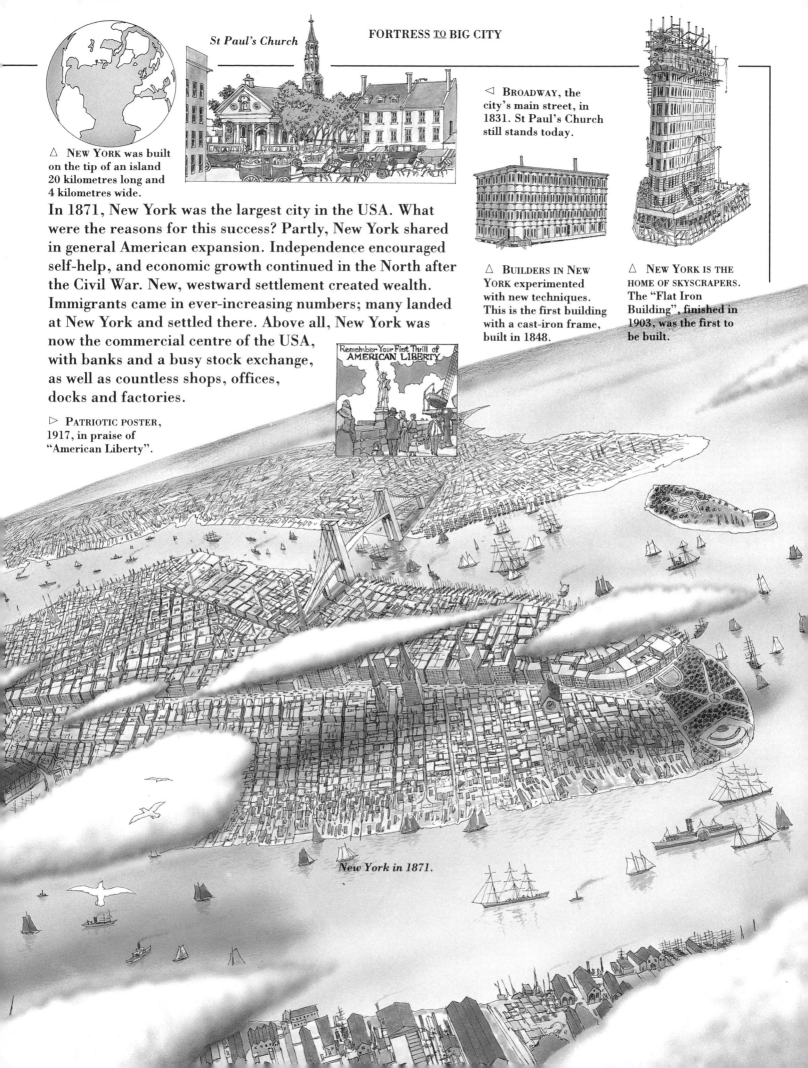

St Paul's Church

△ NEW YORK was built on the tip of an island 20 kilometres long and 4 kilometres wide.

◁ BROADWAY, the city's main street, in 1831. St Paul's Church still stands today.

In 1871, New York was the largest city in the USA. What were the reasons for this success? Partly, New York shared in general American expansion. Independence encouraged self-help, and economic growth continued in the North after the Civil War. New, westward settlement created wealth. Immigrants came in ever-increasing numbers; many landed at New York and settled there. Above all, New York was now the commercial centre of the USA, with banks and a busy stock exchange, as well as countless shops, offices, docks and factories.

▷ PATRIOTIC POSTER, 1917, in praise of "American Liberty".

Remember Your First Thrill of AMERICAN LIBERTY

△ BUILDERS IN NEW YORK experimented with new techniques. This is the first building with a cast-iron frame, built in 1848.

△ NEW YORK IS THE HOME OF SKYSCRAPERS. The "Flat Iron Building", finished in 1903, was the first to be built.

New York in 1871.

INDUSTRIAL CITIES

△ PITTSBURGH is located in the American midwest, near the Great Lakes and coalfields.

WHERE THERE'S MUCK THERE'S BRASS, or so one nineteenth-century factory owner proclaimed. What did he mean? Put simply, he was saying that industry might be dirty, but it was also very profitable. From his own standpoint, he was right. The "steel barons", who controlled enormous factories turning out metal ingots and iron girders, made fortunes in Britain, Europe and the USA. Their goods were needed to make and repair the ingenious machines – from railway locomotives to weaving looms – that brought amazing changes to nineteenth-century cities.

▽ WORKERS' HOUSES were crammed between dirty and dangerous steelworks in 19th-century Pittsburgh. There were no paved streets, drains, water supplies or gardens.

But what about the workers? What impact did the growth of heavy industry have upon their lives? At first, they welcomed it. They hurried to the towns, desperate to find work, and eager to escape from hunger and poverty.

Life in the countryside had been hard. In Ireland, crop failure caused terrible famines. In Britain, many villagers could find only low-paid seasonal work. They also resented their humble social status as tenants of rich families' great estates.

It seemed as if the factories could at last give them the chance to make good money in a steady job. Many poor people from all over Europe emigrated to the USA, in the hopes of a better life in "the land of opportunity".

△ INDUSTRIAL CITIES also developed in 19th-century Europe. This view of Leeds, a British cloth-manufacturing city, reveals smoke, dust and terrible overcrowding.

◁ WOMEN WORKED in appalling conditions to keep their families warm and well fed.

▷ MONSTER LADLES, full of hot metal, tower above workers at the Carnegie Steelworks, Pittsburgh, in 1905.

But, like many dreamers, the workers woke to face reality. Life in industrial cities was bleak. Wages were low; industrial accidents and diseases were common. Housing was terrible and pollution was everywhere.

▷ LOADING COKE, which was needed to make steel, at a coalmine railway terminus near Pittsburgh, c.1870.

LONDON EXPANDS

NINETEENTH-CENTURY LONDON was not just the capital of England; it was also the principal city of the British Empire. After 1857, that included Canada, Australia, New Zealand, India and much of Africa. As imperial capital – and residence of Queen Victoria, one of the most powerful monarchs the world had ever seen – London was home to many influential people. Members of Parliament, military officers, diplomats, colonial administrators, explorers and missionaries all visited London to discuss their policies and seek advice.

△ NEW BUILDINGS for the British Parliament, known as "the Mother of Parliaments". They were designed in a mock-medieval style by the architects Barry and Pugin.

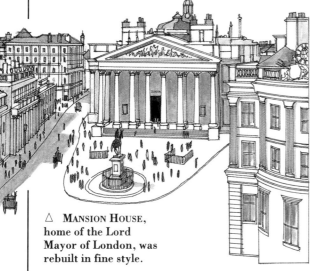

△ MANSION HOUSE, home of the Lord Mayor of London, was rebuilt in fine style.

Many noble families living in the country came regularly to London, to take part in the "Season" – a time of garden parties, dances and dinners that only rich and well-born people were privileged to attend.

▽ PANORAMA OF LONDON, c.1900, a port and capital city.

△ LUXURY GOODS from all around the world on display in Harrods Food Hall, c.1900. Department stores like Harrods served the upper classes of 19th-century London.

34

△ LONDON was built on the lowest crossing point of the wide River Thames, in southeast England.

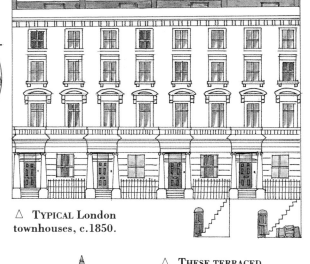

△ TYPICAL London townhouses, c.1850.

△ THESE TERRACED HOUSES had 15 to 20 rooms to house a wealthy family and its servants.

◁ FINE PUBLIC BUILDINGS (this is the Natural History Museum) were built c.1870-80.

△ LONDON attracted a variety of political protesters, like these Suffragettes, c.1910.

The buildings of nineteenth-century London reflect all these upper-class activities. The Houses of Parliament were enlarged, and many new government offices were built. Banks and other financial institutions commissioned new city headquarters. Roomy townhouses could be rented, and furnished with purchases from one of the smart new department stores. Some shops catered specially for the colonial trade and sent boxes of home comforts and tropical kit to distant outposts of the Empire.

△ IN 1899, LONDON had 61 theatres and 39 major music halls. The Savoy Theatre was the first to introduce electric light, in 1881.

◁ HIGH SOCIETY visited London for pleasure. This upper-class young woman was expected to be "an ornament to society", and not to work in trade.

Warehouses

Unloading goods

Barge

Nineteenth-century Londoners were also eager to improve their minds. Encouraged by Prince Albert, husband of Queen Victoria, they built new museums, art galleries and concert halls that are still used today.

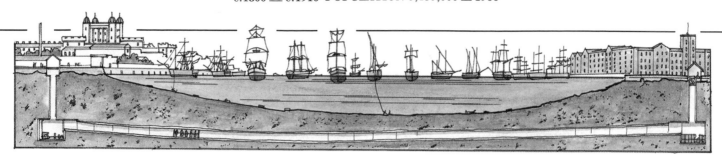

LONDON WORKS

THERE WAS ANOTHER, darker side to nineteenth-century London. The capital of the Empire was also home to thousands of poor and hungry families. Industrial wages were low and housing conditions were grim. Even though London factories promised "light work", this could still be dangerous.

△ THE FIRST LONDON UNDERGROUND train service opened in 1863 to meet the needs of people travelling to work. This shows the first underground railway tunnel dug beneath the River Thames. It brought Londoners living in the southern suburbs close to the commercial heart of the city.

△ BOY selling matches.

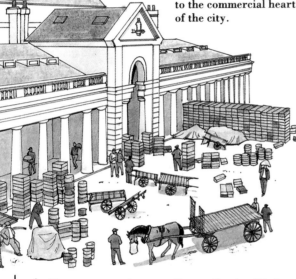

△ FRESH FOOD SUPPLIES were essential for everyone living and working in the city. Covent Garden Market sold flowers, fruit and vegetables brought from the countryside.

▷ WOMEN AND CHILDREN often worked 12-hour shifts in factories to be able to buy food.

Blackfriars Bridge

Passenger steamer

▷ THE PORT OF LONDON handled goods from Europe and from the British Empire, especially foods and raw materials from Africa, Australia, India and the Far East.

◁ THE REVEREND BOOTH'S soup kitchen, c.1876. Many poor Londoners relied on charity for food.

▷ HOUSING FOR THE POOR was dirty and crowded. Many rooms lacked ventilation.

Children worked on the streets – running errands, selling fruit and flowers, or sweeping the roads clean of horse droppings. Until the 1870s, when free education was provided by the state, many could not read or write. This limited their chances of finding a well-paid job and breaking free from a life of hardship and poverty. Some wealthy, well-meaning Londoners were horrified by this underworld. They set up charitable schemes to provide free food and shelter for London's poor.

△ THESE WORKERS' HOUSES, close to a noisy overhead railway line, were first criticised by the artist and social reformer Gustave Doré in the 1870s.

△ THERE WERE FEW bathrooms and lavatories. People shared a cold-water pipe in the common yard, and built a "privy" in the garden.

△ SMOKE AND SOOT in the air caused choking London smog.

▽ THE DOCKS were crowded with cranes and warehouses, and the river was full of ships.

St Paul's Cathedral

Tower Bridge

Tugboat

Dredger

But not all Londoners were rich or poor. The majority lived modestly, earning a living in pubs, cafes, shops and offices, or in the rougher, noisier, markets and docks. To get there, they travelled by horse-drawn omnibus or the new Underground, which opened in 1863. After work, the men might go to the local pub or take their families to the music hall to enjoy clowns, songs and comedy acts.

OUT OF TOWN

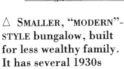

△ THIS POSTER advertises "Metroland" – areas outside London that could be reached by Underground.

FOR MANY PEOPLE, city life was hard. They faced pollution, overcrowding and noise. In the late nineteenth century, politicians and architects began to look for a solution. They improved living conditions by building homes, schools and hospitals. They arranged better sewage, refuse collections and clean water. Zoning separated industrial and residential areas. But these measures could not solve overcrowding, and the disease and crime it brought. So new suburbs and healthy "garden cities" were planned.

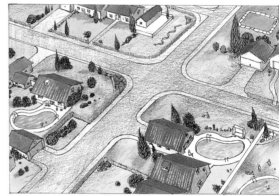

◁ LONDON TRANSPORT built many new Underground stations during the 1920s and 1930s, in a distinctive, modern style. Travelling by "Tube" was advertised as comfortable, fast, easy and cheap. In other cities throughout the world, travellers made similar daily journeys to work by subway or small, local railway.

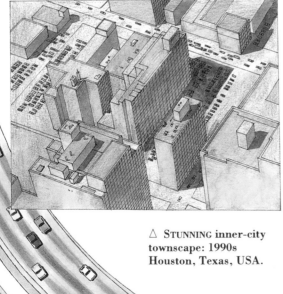

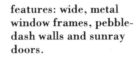

△ LARGE, TUDOR-STYLE house, built in 1920 for the prosperous suburban middle class.

△ SMALLER, "MODERN"-STYLE bungalow, built for less wealthy family. It has several 1930s features: wide, metal window frames, pebble-dash walls and sunray doors.

△ IN THIS RICH SUBURB of Seattle, Washington, USA, c.1980, almost every house has a pool.

▽ SHANTY TOWNS provide homes for poor people who move to big cities in search of work.

△ STUNNING inner-city townscape: 1990s Houston, Texas, USA.

△ EARNING A LIVING from the city's waste: these men are recycling old oil cans to make lamps in Cairo, Egypt.

Living out of town had advantages. Land was cheaper, so houses could be larger, with space for children to play.
But not all suburbs are clean and comfortable. Some cities today are surrounded by squalid shanty towns.

MOTORWAY MADNESS? ▷

INNER CITY

IN CITIES TODAY, great poverty exists alongside tremendous wealth. This is not a new problem; it has troubled most cities in the past. Cities attract homeless and unemployed people, because they offer the chance to make a fresh start. Many cities have tried to combat poverty. In Rome, emperors gave "bread and circuses". In the USA in the nineteenth century, people were urged "to pull themselves up by their own bootstraps", while in the 1960s, China shared out surplus goods. Today, most European states provide welfare benefits, but the problem remains unsolved.

△ IN MANY CITIES, traffic can no longer move freely.

▽ HOMELESS PEOPLE resort to "cardboard cities" for shelter.

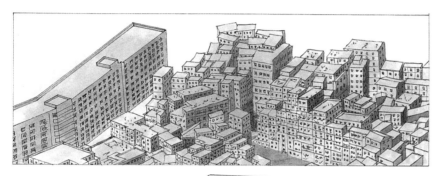

△ THE "WALLED CITY" area of Kowloon, Hong Kong, which was demolished in 1991 because it was so dangerous. The fragile, homemade skyscrapers were home to 33,000 people. The streets were so narrow it was difficult for people to pass. The only place for children to play was 14 floors up, on the slippery roof.

It is easy to feel alone and helpless in a big city if you are far from family and friends. Overcrowding leads to fear and aggression, while decay, caused by vandalism, neglect, or poverty, increases feelings of despair.

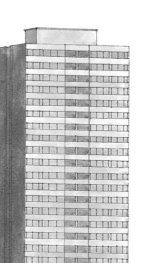

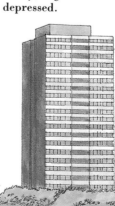

HIGH-RISE FLATS were praised by architects of the 1950s. But now they are criticised. People living there often feel lonely, frightened and depressed.

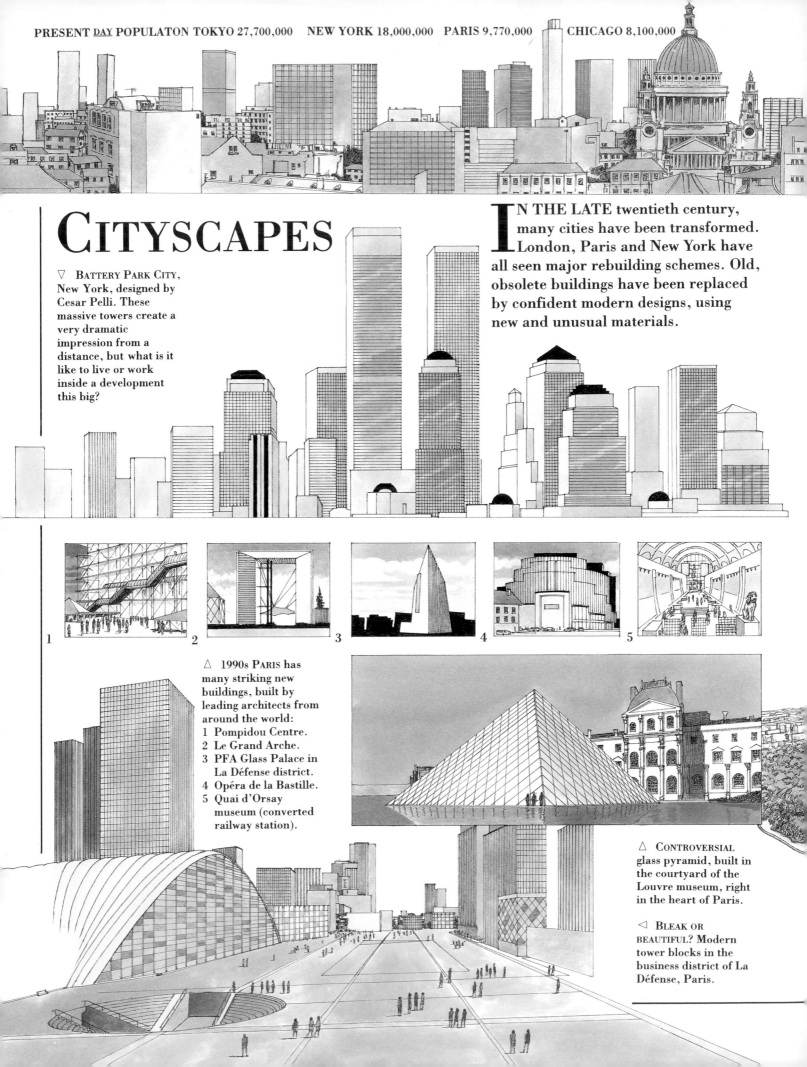

CITYSCAPES

▽ BATTERY PARK CITY, New York, designed by Cesar Pelli. These massive towers create a very dramatic impression from a distance, but what is it like to live or work inside a development this big?

IN THE LATE twentieth century, many cities have been transformed. London, Paris and New York have all seen major rebuilding schemes. Old, obsolete buildings have been replaced by confident modern designs, using new and unusual materials.

1   2   3   4   5

△ 1990s PARIS has many striking new buildings, built by leading architects from around the world:
1 Pompidou Centre.
2 Le Grand Arche.
3 PFA Glass Palace in La Défense district.
4 Opéra de la Bastille.
5 Quai d'Orsay museum (converted railway station).

△ CONTROVERSIAL glass pyramid, built in the courtyard of the Louvre museum, right in the heart of Paris.

◁ BLEAK OR BEAUTIFUL? Modern tower blocks in the business district of La Défense, Paris.

CAIRO 9,300,000 SHANGHAI 9,300,000 BEIJING 7,320,000   LONDON 11,000,000 CALCUTTA 9,200,000 MOSCOW 8,820,000

△ LONDON BEFORE THE 1980s. The skyline is dominated by the 17th-century dome of St Paul's Cathedral. Today, high-rise buildings blot out the former view.

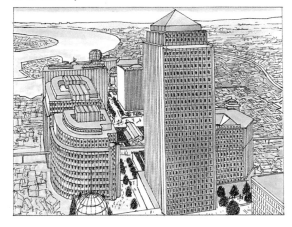

△ MODERN architecture is not always admired. The Canary Wharf scheme in London's Docklands (*above*) has been criticised by the Prince of Wales. He feels that Canary Wharf's tower, which is two and a half times taller than St Paul's, ruins the London skyline.

New building techniques have had a dramatic effect on how cities look. All architects have wanted to leave their mark on the world. But it is now possible for one designer to have an enormous impact on a city and the people who live there. Twentieth-century architecture is bigger, bolder and, perhaps, more "brutal" than anything built in the past.

Architects can now construct offices, public buildings and blocks of flats that are quite unrelated to natural or human scales. They are taller than any tree, and hard for individual men and women to feel at home with. They are also impossible to ignore. Some critics say that they ruin city landscapes by overpowering all that was there before.

Yet many of these new buildings, made of steel and concrete and coated with reflective glass, are stunningly beautiful. In the "right" setting (as part of a whole new town, maybe, or planned with consideration for the local environment), vast modern constructions can be as awe-inspiring and exciting as any great building of the past.

Modern city buildings owe their striking good looks to new materials used in imaginative ways. For example, many new buildings rely on specially coated steel panels first developed for use in space.

▷ THE "NEW" CITY of Sydney, Australia, is proud of its many modern buildings.

◁ SYDNEY OPERA HOUSE, completed in the 1970s. An original design praised for its dramatic use of a stunning natural site.

41

FUTURE CITIES

W HAT PROBLEMS will face architects designing cities of the future? From our own place in history, we can only guess, but it is likely that many of today's problems will still be causing difficulties in the future. Pollution, overcrowding and crime are among the most serious problems facing present-day cities. Some scientists might also add the possibility of climatic change, or the high levels of psychological stress found among city-dwellers, brought about by isolation and fear.

△ AN EXTRATERRESTRIAL CITY orbits in space. Shuttle flights link it with earth.

▽ CITY ON THE MOON, protected from the inhospitable climate by a bubble.

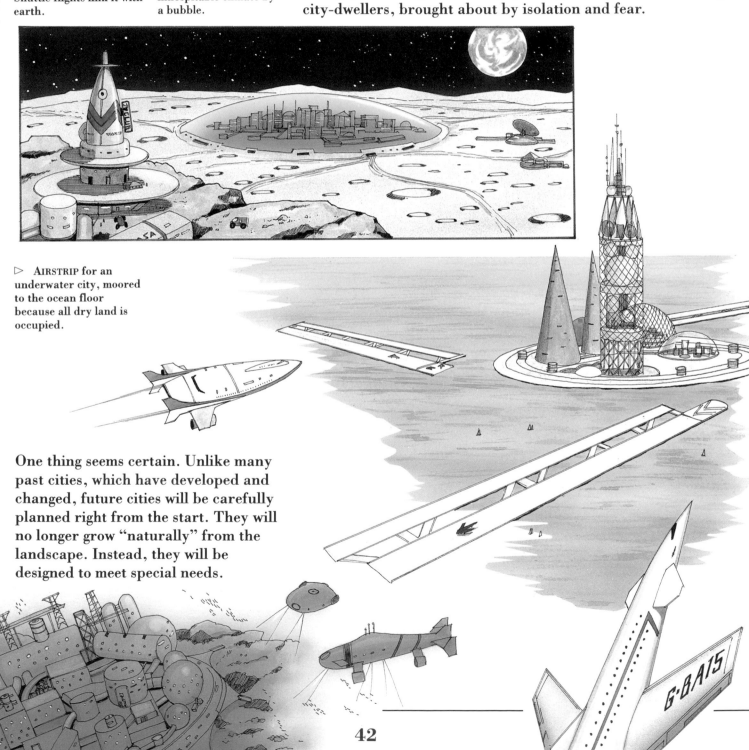

▷ AIRSTRIP for an underwater city, moored to the ocean floor because all dry land is occupied.

One thing seems certain. Unlike many past cities, which have developed and changed, future cities will be carefully planned right from the start. They will no longer grow "naturally" from the landscape. Instead, they will be designed to meet special needs.

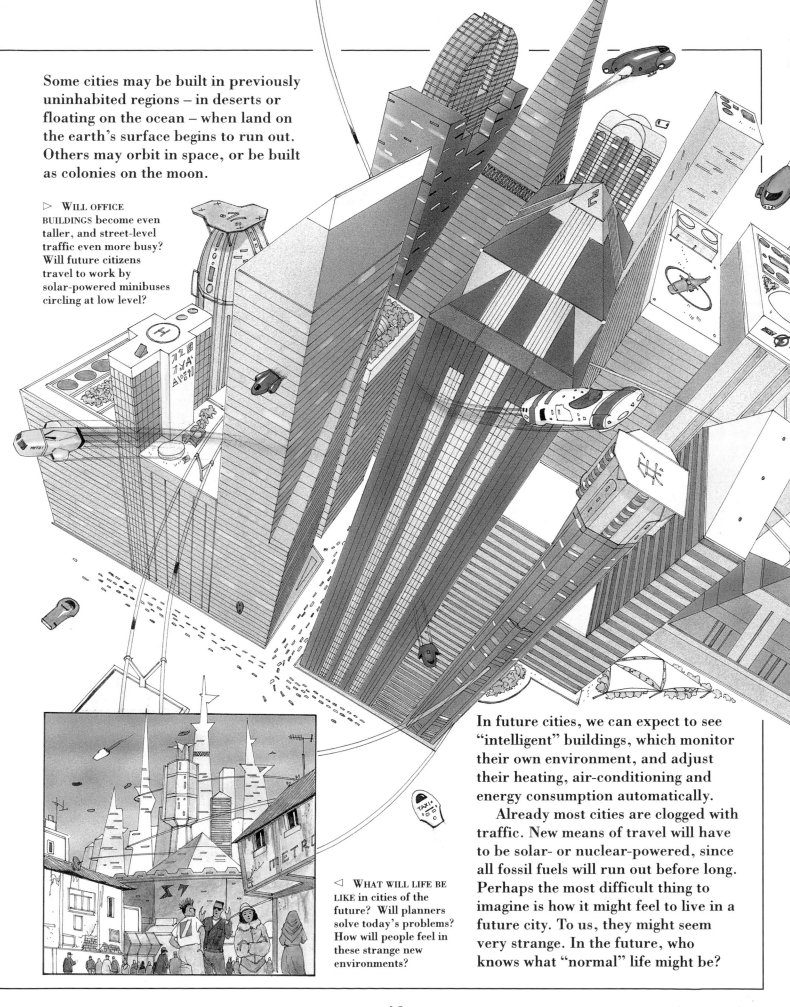

Some cities may be built in previously uninhabited regions – in deserts or floating on the ocean – when land on the earth's surface begins to run out. Others may orbit in space, or be built as colonies on the moon.

▷ WILL OFFICE BUILDINGS become even taller, and street-level traffic even more busy? Will future citizens travel to work by solar-powered minibuses circling at low level?

◁ WHAT WILL LIFE BE LIKE in cities of the future? Will planners solve today's problems? How will people feel in these strange new environments?

In future cities, we can expect to see "intelligent" buildings, which monitor their own environment, and adjust their heating, air-conditioning and energy consumption automatically.

Already most cities are clogged with traffic. New means of travel will have to be solar- or nuclear-powered, since all fossil fuels will run out before long. Perhaps the most difficult thing to imagine is how it might feel to live in a future city. To us, they might seem very strange. In the future, who knows what "normal" life might be?

43

TIMELINE

Sumerian merchants

The Incas of Peru

BC

c.8350-7350 First large towns built in Middle East, for example, Jericho, which covered 10 acres.

c.6250-5400 The first known city – Catal Huyuk (in present-day Turkey). At its richest and most powerful it covered 32 acres.

c.3500 The first Chinese city built at Liang Ch'eng Chen.

c.3000 Cities like Ur and Sumer built in the "Fertile Crescent" region (present-day Syria and Iraq).

c.2685 Powerful Old Kingdom established in Egypt, with its capital city at Memphis.

Egyptian temple

c.2500 First cities built in Indus Valley region (present-day India and Pakistan).

c.2000 Rich palace-city at Knossos on the Mediterranean island of Crete. Controls a sea-based empire.

c.1750 Empire based in the city of Babylon (in present-day Iraq) rises to power under King Hammurabi.

Athenian fishmonger

c.1600 Rich cities flourish under the Shang emperors in China.

c.1567 New Kingdom established in Egypt; capital city moved to Thebes. "City of the dead" built nearby.

c.1370 Pharaoh Akenhaten builds new city dedicated to the Spirit of the Sun at Tell-el-Amarna in central Egypt. It is abandoned shortly after his death.

c.1000 King David, leader of the Jewish people, establishes a new temple in the city of Jerusalem.

c.814 The great trading city of Carthage is set up on the north African coast. It later rules over a kingdom.

753 According to legend, the date when Rome was founded.

c.750 The first Greek city-states rise to power.

c.510 The beginning of republican government in Rome.

c.505 The beginning of democracy in Athens.

c.500-c.400 The "golden age" of art and architecture in Athens. Literature and philosophy also

Roman sculpture

flourish. Under the leadership of Pericles (died 429 BC), Athens becomes the most powerful state in Greece.

c.322 The city of Magadha becomes the centre of the new Mauryan empire in India.

c.202 New Chinese capital city built at Changan.

c.100 First settlement appears on the site of present-day Paris.

AD

27 Roman Empire begins.

c.132 Areas of Jerusalem destroyed after the Jewish people rebel against Roman rule.

c.300 Mayan peoples build cities in the rainforests of Guatemala. Beginning of powerful city-states in Mexico, at Monte Alban and Teotihuacan. By AD 600, Teotihuacan has over 125,000 inhabitants.

632 The city of Mecca becomes a place of pilgrimage for Muslim people from all over the world.

794 New Japanese capital city founded at Kyoto.

c.700-800 Baghdad (in present-day Iraq) becomes the most important city in the Muslim world. Under its ruler Caliph Harun al-Rashid, it becomes a great centre of art and learning. It is also immensely rich.

862 Viking traders, led by Rurik, found the city of Novgorod in the north of Russia.

969 The Famitid dynasty conquers Egypt and establishes the new city of Cairo near the mouth of the River Nile.

c.1000 Settlement begins at the site of the great city of Zimbabwe, in Africa. The inhabitants grow rich through raising cattle and mining gold.

c.1100 The Toltecs build a large city to be the capital of their kingdom at Tula, in present-day Mexico.

c.1150 Great temple cities, for example, Angkor Wat, are built in Southeast Asia.

c.1200 City-states of the Yoruba and Hausa peoples become powerful in western Africa (in present-day Nigeria and the neighbouring lands).

c.1206 Muslim Sultanate (kingdom) of Delhi founded in India. Over the next 300 years, it rules over a large territory and is famous for its wealth.

c.1336-1565 The city of Vijayanagar controls a large territory in southern India. Visitors marvel at its fine architecture and the way it is planned to provide a cool environment in the hot, tropical climate.

Playing chess in Córdoba

c.1364 The Aztec capital city of Tenochtitlán founded on the shores of a great lake in central Mexico. The inhabitants plant "floating gardens" in the marshes nearby, to grow food.

London in 1900

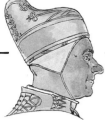

Giovanni Mocenigo

c.1400-c.1500 Artists and philosophers produce important works in the cities of Renaissance Italy.

1421 The Chin rulers of China make Peking (present-day Beijing) their new capital city. They build a great palace there, known as the "forbidden city", because only the Emperor, his family and servants can enter. Peking remains the capital of China until 1911.

1453 Constantinople (present-day Istanbul) is conquered by Muslim

Palazzo Davanatzi

troops loyal to the Ottoman sultans of Turkey. It becomes the new capital of the strong Ottoman empire.

c.1500-c.1700 Amsterdam, in the Netherlands, becomes the largest and most profitable port in Europe.

1509 The first watch is

made by Peter Henle, a metalworker from Nuremberg.

1598 The beautiful city of Isfahan (in present-day Iran) becomes the capital of a new Persian empire.

1618 Dutch merchants set up a trading city at Batavia, in the East Indies. From there, cloth and spices are shipped back to Europe.

1626 Dutch settlers found a fort on Manhattan Island, now part of New York.

1642 French explorers establish the first European city in Canada, at Ville-Marie, now called Montreal.

1652 Dutch explorers set up a town in Cape Colony, South Africa, which later grows into the important city of Cape Town.

1665 Many Londoners die in the last major outbreak of bubonic plague to affect Britain.

1666 Large areas of the old city are destroyed in the Great Fire of London.

1703 St Petersburg founded by the Russian Tsar Peter the Great.

1718 New Orleans is the first city to be built in what would become the southern states of the USA.

1788 Settlement begins at the first colonial cities in Australia.

1789-99 The city of Paris is thrown into confusion during the French Revolution and the years that follow. Many people killed, including the king,

Seal of Amsterdam

Louis XVI, who is executed along with many other members of the royal family.

1790 The city of Washington, DC, becomes federal capital of the USA.

1849 The city of San Francisco grows rapidly during the "Gold Rush", when miners rush to look for gold in the hills nearby.

1853 Baron Haussmann begins his grand scheme to rebuild Paris.

Flat Iron Building

1863 The first underground railway is built in London, allowing city dwellers to travel longer distances to work, and helping cities to grow even bigger.

1874 The first electric railway opens in New

York. Like travel by Underground, fast, cheap electric transport encourages cities to expand.

1879 F.W. Woolworth opens the first "5 and 10 cent stores" in American cities, selling cheap goods to city workers.

1887-89 The Eiffel Tower is completed for the celebrations of the centenary (100 year anniversary) of the French Revolution.

1888 The Statue of Liberty, a gift to the American people from the French, is installed on Bedloe Island, in the Hudson River, off New York City.

1889 The town planner E. Howard publishes the book *Garden Cities of Tomorrow*, the first book devoted to planning cities that would be healthy and attractive to live in. It has a great influence in Britain and Europe, and several new Garden Cities are planned.

1892 Ellis Island, off New York City, opens as the chief immigration station for the USA.

1906 Large areas of San Francisco, USA, are destroyed by an earthquake. Scientists predict that another major earthquake may occur in the future.

1945 The Japanese cities of Hiroshima and Nagasaki are the first to be devastated by atomic bombs. Many of their citizens are

killed, and others die later from illness caused by atomic radiation.

1946 New York is chosen to be the headquarters of the United Nations, founded after the Second World War to try to maintain world peace.

1948 Israel founded with a new capital city at Tel Aviv.

1957 Brussels, in Belgium, chosen to house the headquarters of the European Economic Community, or "Common Market" (now known as the European Community).

c.1960-90 New high-rise building schemes in major cities throughout the world.

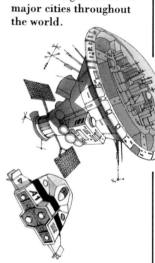

Extraterrestrial city

1990 The city of Berlin in Germany is reunified. The Berlin Wall, which had divided it since 1961, is torn down, watched by enthusiastic crowds.

GLOSSARY

Access To reach.

Aqueduct Raised channel carrying water to a city. Often looks like a high bridge.

Alliances Friendships.

Amenities Useful things.

Antique Very old. Often used to refer to the world of Ancient Greece and Rome, from the years c.800 BC - AD c.500.

Archeologists People who study the remains of the past.

Arena Large open space, usually with seating all around.

Asia Minor Present-day Turkey and neighbouring territories in the USSR.

Caliph Leader of a Muslim state.

Civic Belonging to a city.

Climatic change Long-term changes in the weather.

Colony Land taken over and administered by a foreign state.

Corpse Dead body.

Cremation The practice of burning dead bodies, rather than burying them.

Democracy A system of government in which all adult citizens (or, in the past, men) can vote and influence policy.

Discreet Quiet and not boastful.

Dominated Controlled; governed.

Dynasty Ruling family.

Elected Chosen by vote.

Emigrate Choose to leave your home country to seek a better life abroad.

Empire A number of different countries all ruled by one powerful state.

Encircled Surrounded.

Epidemic Disease that attacks a large number of people at the same time.

Eternal Lasting forever; endless.

Financial institutions Companies such as banks and insurance companies that make profits by lending and investing money.

Fortified With strong defences, for example, walls and gates.

Girders Strong metal bars used in buildings and for making modern ships.

Humanist Concerned with people and their achievements, rather than with God.

Immigrants People coming to settle in a new land.

Imperial Ruling an empire.

Ingot Blocks of high-quality metal, used to make tools and machines.

Intact Undamaged.

Intrigue Plots or conspiracies.

Khan A ruler in China from the 13th to the 15th centuries, after the invasion by Mongol peoples from Central Asia.

Manuscript Document written by hand.

Massive Heavy, solid and very big.

Molten Melted to become liquid.

Mummified Preserved by drying with chemicals, then wrapping in bandages soaked in oils, herbs and spices. Many mummies still survive from Egyptian times.

Muslim Someone who worships God following the example set by the Prophet Muhammad (died AD 632) and the teachings of the holy book known as the Qu'ran.

Notorious Famous for being bad.

Omnibus The old name for a bus or coach carrying a large number of people. It is a Latin word, meaning "(used) by all".

Ottoman The name of a Turkish dynasty that was powerful from the 15th to the 19th centuries. Also used to describe the empire it ruled.

Patrons People who give money to support the arts or other good causes.

Philosopher Someone who studies the best way to live (and other important questions, as well).

Protestant A member of one of the churches that broke away from the Catholic church during the 16th century after protests by religious leaders like Martin Luther and Jean Calvin.

Provision merchants People selling food.

Psychological stress Worry and depression.

Ramparts High banks of earth used for defence.

Republic A system of government without a royal family. Instead, there is an elected head of state, like the President of the USA today.

Sanitation Sewers, drains and fresh drinking water supplies.

Solar Coming from the sun.

Squalid Dirty and unhealthy.

Stock Exchange A place where stocks and bonds are traded by stockbrokers, who buy part-shares in companies for other people.

Suburbs Areas on the edge of a city.

Surplus Extra; more than you need.

Traditional Following a long-established way of doing something.

Tropical kit Clothes suitable for wearing in hot climates.

Tsar The Russian word for king or emperor (from the Latin "Caesar").

Turmoil Upheaval, unrest.

Zoning Dividing a city into areas limited to a particular use, like housing or heavy industry.

INDEX

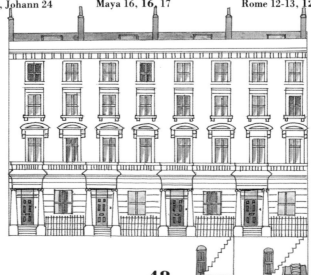